Learn**English**
WithAfrica

SHORT STORY

The Pinnacle Of Irresponsibility

LEVEL B1-B2

Reading Comprehension and Vocabulary Worksheets

By
Thandi Ngwira Gatignol

CONTENTS

FOREWORD

There are many advantages to reading short stories when you are learning English.

First of all, short stories are 'short', therefore you a get a sense of accomplishment much quicker than when you read a novel.

Secondly, you encounter different interesting characters and you can put yourself in their shoes. This can be done by appropriating the way they think or talk. Vocabulary is thus easier to grasp and digest.

Thirdly, language and grammatical structures are seen in context. Hence, you will gain a deeper understanding of how words, tenses and punctuation work together to form meaning.

Finally, reading short stories gives you access to valuable cultural information about a people, country or continent.

I hope that ***The Pinnacle of Irresponsibility*** meets your expectations and fosters your own creativity.

Thandi Ngwira Gatignol, Founder (Learn English With Africa)

The Pinnacle of Irresponsibility

He was the fifth child that my uncle dumped on me. Dogs announced his coming; the night guard shoved him into our compound.

"This thief claims to be your nephew."

The boy dropped onto the ground as soon as he saw me. He whimpered when his bare knees grazed the gravel. There was a trail of blood behind him and his soaked clothes bore witness to what he'd just been through. I wondered if it was the work of our Rottweiler or *a*Phiri's own doing.

"Put that dog away."

*A*Phiri pretended not to have heard me. He instead tightened his grip on the boy's swollen wrist while the left hand held the leash that kept Kobra in place.

"Put that dog away."

"Sir..."

"He's not lying."

"Please sir..."

"He is my nephew," I insisted.

"Sir!"

The hard edge in *a*Phiri's voice jostled my complacency.

"APhiri! Do as I say. You have never disobeyed me before. Take your bloody hands off that boy!"

Slowly, like a snake unhooking its fangs from a prey, the guard's fingers unfurled, revealing a red palm that hurt my eyes as much as they had bruised the little boy's wrist.

"Coward," *a*Phiri erupted. "You should never have a faint heart when it comes to these people."

The boy cringed as the older man reached out for his wrist again. I shook my head.

"No pity sir. Do not be fooled by his chicken legs. His friends are hiding there." APhiri's sharp elbow pointed at a flimsy row of bare-leafed hedges that bordered a part of our house. "These dogs have no pity. None at all. They will strip you and your house naked and believe me they won't have any pinch of remorse. You should never let a dog enter your house or it will forget its place. Treat a dog like a human being and it will become one. This is how you should treat these dogs."

Turning towards the boy, *a*Phiri spat his anger out, and I watched helplessly as the blob of colourful spittle landed on my nephew's head. A thin dusty hand rose to wipe the sticky intrusion away. The bigger hand clasped the offering in its grip again as Kobra whined and dag under his feet with frantic strokes, sniffing at the clods of earth in hungry anticipation.

For a few seconds I watched the scene with fascination like a spectator of a Discovery Channel documentary. The boy writhed in pain while silent tears watered the ground beneath him. My fascination turned into dismay when I realised that *a*Phiri's zeal was fuelled by the boy's strangled groans. The more the boy struggled, the more *a*Phiri unleashed his power, crushing his game until the muscles in his strong arms gave away.

When he was satisfied, *a*Phiri brushed the front of his uniform, removing thin blades of grass that were coated with a dark mixture of earth and human fluid. The unwanted particles fell near his feet, remnants of a rather bizarre feast in which he was the sole guest.

"Go away!" he howled. My eyes swarmed with visions of neighbours storming our compound, branding panga knives and sticks, thirsty for revenge. The most irate of them would be wielding car tyres and fuel, aching to erase the existence of somebody who had dared violate the privacy of their material world. Meanwhile, the dog kicked and griped, ready to pounce.

"Go away or today you'll know what shaved the guinea fowl."

"He...he... can't move. Your hands are too ti...tight." I found myself stuttering.

"Shut up."

His words were like a punch right through my chest. I staggered under the weight of their consequences. I had employed *a*Phiri to protect my family. There was no way I would live in the shadow of his threats. A long silence ensued as I tried to find the right words that would shake him out of his lunacy.

"Listen..."

"Sir, don't be like a mad person. These people make our lives miserable."

As if taking a cue from the tone of his master, the dog started barking and tugging on the leash. APhiri was forced to let go of the boy's wrist as he wrestled with

Kobra. I instinctively grabbed the freed hand and dashed to the verandah before the boy and I became the unwitting dish of a bloodthirsty pair.

"Open the door!" I banged on the glass panes that were shielded from prying hands with burglars' bars. "*Nya*Kayira*we*, please open the door."

"What's happening *ŵa*Gondwe? What's this ruckus? People are sleeping for Christ's sake." She towered above my head and saw the bleeding boy cowering behind my back. "Oh God, we're being attacked by armed robbers again."

She retreated in haste and disappeared from my view. I rattled at the glassy door in nervous rasps. I waited, resting my sweaty head on the icy metal that barred me from entering my own house. I had the strange hope that my children would hear me and come to our rescue. I could hear Kobra's and *a*Phiri's barking receding in the distance. I waited.

Twack! I shuddered at the sound. Its regular cadence numbed any reaction I would have had in similar circumstances. Twack! Twack! Twack! In the end, it was the muffled whimpering that alerted me. My head rose from the door in painful motions. I clasped my eyes tight as the thumping behind me alternated with the crying of a wounded animal in the throes of distress.

"Go back where you came from!" It was my wife's voice and I turned. In her hands was a thick pestle that she used to pound maize in the mortar.

"*Nya*Kayira, what are you doing here? Have you gone crazy?" My admonishment rushed our out in torrents. "You'll kill the child with that thing." I removed the weapon from her hands with unbridled energy. I was surprised that she'd released it without a fight.

"You have a soft heart *ŵa*Gondwe. You will be dead before you know it. Treat these things with leniency and they will bite the very hand that patted them on the back."

She unwrapped her *chitenje* and threw it onto the polished floor, next to the boy who lay in a foetal position, his limp hands clenching a piece of paper that I hadn't noticed before. The fabric partially covered his bare feet which were scarred and mangled. I picked up the *chitenje* and pulled it over the entire length of his lean body.

When I straightened my back to face my wife, she stared at me as if I had just given all my life's savings to an ex-girlfriend. Shaking her head in disbelief, she removed a pair of keys from her bra and thrust the front door open. "If he comes in here, I'll pack my bags and go to my mother's." The bang that followed made my heart leap.

After a few seconds, I knelt beside the boy and unclenched his fist slowly. I took the piece of smeared paper and started reading its contents.

Goodson Gondwe,
Kanena Village,
T/A Nthumbonjikuru,
P.O Box 7,
Rumphi.

Dear son,

I have given you another present to increase the wealth of your household. His name is Vinjeru. He is the son of your eldest sister who now lives in Chitipa.

He can be a good houseboy. I swear on the body of my dead mother that this goat will never give you any trouble. If he does, he will be as good as a dead dog.

I know that you have done a good job with the previous children I sent you, praise God, they are all doing well in their private schools.

I must say that I did my best in instilling a sense of duty in your thick skull. Thanks to my continuous efforts as advisor and breadwinner of the family, you landed yourself the job that you now have today. You should always remember that.

The economic situation is not good here.

The bale of sugar that you sent us last time is almost gone. I do not know how I will manage with no tea in the morning. Please share with us village people the little you have so that we may prosper like you for we all live under the same sun and we were created by the same God.

I am not asking for the Benz that you ride to work. No, no, no. It is of no use to me. But remember that your feet once raked the same soil I walk on every day and they may do so again. Remember that. I am not asking for bread and butter either. Those are the things that people from town eat. I no longer have any teeth anyway so that is not necessary for me but remember that your employer could fire you and you would have to come back to the village with your whole family. What will you feed them with?

Vinjeru is now yours. I give him to you, freely. You can do whatever you want with him and I will not raise a hand.

Please send the telegram as soon as possible.

In Jesus's name I sign off.

Goodson Gondwe

Proud owner of Gondwe and Sons' Investments

P.S. Your mother is complaining of her rheumatism as usual. Send us some medicine if you have some. Panadol will be all right as a painkiller. We village people are not choosers. Send us anything and we will take it. GOD BLESS YOU MY SON.

I glanced at Vinjeru. I had never seen him before. My elder cousin had left home when I was still at secondary school. She had eloped with a man who was much older than her and we never saw her again. We only heard from her when trouble came knocking at her door. I wondered if she knew about my uncle's plans and if she'd dared counter them. Perhaps she had goaded him into sending this child seeing that I had taken care of the four others without protest.

"Does your mother know that you are here?"

A grunt escaped from Vinjeru's lips as he curled further into himself. I stood up and banged on the door again.

Our housemaid drew the curtains and stared at my bloodstained hands with disgust and a little fear.

"Ask Mummy to come!" I shouted but she could not hear me. I repeated my plea.

Nambewe chose to open the window instead but made sure to keep her head away from the foul air.

"Can you please ask Mummy to come?"

"She said that I shouldn't open the door."

"I didn't ask you to open the door. I asked you to tell Mummy to come here."

"But Daddy, Mummy said that I shouldn't open the door for anyone, especially for that thing." She pointed in horror at the figure that lay prostrated on the ground. "But Daddy, why are you wasting your time with that thing? Just leave it alone. It will die anyway as soon as we toss it outside the gate." She closed the window and hid her view from me as the curtains closed down upon us.

I had to think fast. I fumbled in my pockets and found the car keys that I had forgotten to take out of my pockets the previous evening. Lately, I had started working overtime in order to manage with the financial demands that were thrust upon my 35-year old shoulders. I worked as a Senior Accountant for a private law firm but even the hefty salary that I got from this job was not sufficient enough to cover all my household's expenses and those extra ones that usually came at unexpected times. Perhaps time would come when I would have to leave the country to go abroad so I could earn Pounds or Dollars that could be easily transformed into thousands of Kwachas. As for now, the only option lay in hard work or in bribes. I chose the first but I knew that it would not take long before I succumbed to the effortless seduction of the latter.

"We will go back to Kanena."

The boy shook his head vigorously, letting out painful groans that I could not understand. I preferred his silence. It forced me to remain in a state of inaction and comforted me that I was doing the right thing in a hard situation.

"*Wadada* will understand." I placed my hand on Vinjeru's back but he recoiled from it.

I watched his body squirm in endless convulsions and I quickly wrenched my eyes from this horrible sight. Of all the people on earth, why did God put me in this position?

I worked hard and did what I could to take care of a large family. No one could accuse me of being a bad father. So why was I being treated this way? Life was indeed tough; my grandmother had warned me. No one chooses their own destiny, she often repeated. Destiny chooses you. She was right. Destiny had chosen me that day and I had to do something.

This had to stop, I told myself. Why should I be the one to bear all these burdens when some people are enjoying themselves without lifting any finger? It was time my uncle knew what I really thought about his presents. My mind was clouded with sudden anger that my sole goal was to embark on this distasteful quest.

I had enough money in the car for the round trip so fuel wouldn't be a problem.

I picked Vinjeru and packed him in the back of my Mercedes. I entered the car and turned on the engine. The crunch of the gravel pierced into my ears as I headed towards the exit. I stopped in front of the metal gate, waiting for *a*Phiri to open it. He was nowhere in sight. Neither was Kobra. I scrambled out of the car and opened the gate myself before jumping back onto the safety of my seat and locking the door immediately. I drove off in a huff and prayed that the 500 Km would not wear me down.

We only stopped twice. Once to buy Fanta and some biscuits for our breakfast. I took it under the shade of a mango tree but Vinjeru could barely open his mouth let alone feed himself properly so the plastic bag of food lay next to him, unwanted and unmaimed. The second time was when I retched on a side road near Kasungu when my nose could no longer handle the smell of the boy's wounds. During this stop, I also called *Nya*Kayira to let her know about our departure.

"I thought you'd taken the boy to Queen Elizabeth Central Hospital."

I didn't know how to answer her so I told her that I would call her back as soon as we arrived in Rumphi. She hung up before I said anything else.

After this incident, we rode in an unbroken silence, occasionally disturbed by Vinjeru's moaning and my own coughs as I tried to cover his suffering. The knocking in my heart also bothered me, especially when we neared our destination. The truth was I was afraid of my uncle and I was not the only one.

Rumphi was reached in late afternoon. The main road leading to the cluster of mud-thatched homes that composed Kanena Village was filled mostly with women and children carrying buckets of water or bundles of firewood. They hurried home, grateful that the imminent sunset would give them the opportunity to finally rest.

I hooted at a stray dog which was crossing the road in a senseless charge. I finally stopped to let the mad dog pass. The thought of hitting that thing and having to eye the contents of its belly sickened me.

The car started moving again and I heard Vinjeru move as his body responded to the changes in the rhythm.

"We are home," he mumbled. I looked at him and smiled but his face was emotionless. And even if he had wanted to smile back, he wouldn't have been able to. His head looked like a mixture of different types of mangoes pasted together to form a grotesque whole. My uncle's wife would take care of him. I was really glad to be at the end of my ordeal.

"Benz! Benz!" a crowd of excited children with distended bellies and dirty tattered clothes ran after my car as I drove up the mud road that led to Goodson Gondwe's house. I slowed down and let the car glide to the verandah of the biggest hut. I struggled my way out as eager hands outside fought to give me the first handshake.

"What should we carry for you?" One boy already ran to the back of the Mercedes to open the boot.

I shrugged my shoulders in shame and told them that I hadn't brought anything. "I didn't have enough time."

"So what's the use of having a beautiful car then?" They laughed and scattered in different directions.

"Oh, my dear boy from town! What brings you hear my boy? How is Blantyre?"

I saw Goodson Gondwe himself advancing towards the car. "I see that you still have your Benz. Ah, I always told you that you would become someone. Even when you didn't have any shoes like those boys you just pushed away." He grabbed my hand and shook it with such warmth that I forgot my former misgivings.

"What have you brought us son?"

"No, nothing uncle. Unfortunately, I did not have enough time." Inwardly, I beat myself for not having bought anything at Jenda roadblock. I would have made my uncle happy for once.

"Ah son, you came all this way with nothing for your ageing father. Empty hands son. No tomatoes. No onions. What happened?"

As I looked for an explanation, I suddenly remembered Vinjeru and the reason why I had travelled all the way from Blantyre to Rumphi. Words failed me. I coughed and pointed at the back of the car.

"Is this a new Benz?"

"No, it's Vinjeru."

"What about him? He's giving you trouble already! I knew that boy was useless." He went to peer at the laying figure in the car. "Useless," he hissed and spat on the ground. "He went all the way to Blantyre only to come back a week later. What happened?"

This was harder than I'd imagined.

"Let's talk on the verandah," I said.

"Ok. I'll take care of that goat in the back as soon as those boys are back. He will remember me for the rest of his life after I've caned him so hard he will no longer be able to sit on his bottom. He can even bleed to death. I don't care."

When I sat down, one of the girls who had been staring at me and giggling from a short distance brought me a glass of water. She knelt and waited to take the plastic tumbler back.

"Give her some money so she can go and buy you some Coca-Cola," my uncle ordered. Meekly, I reached out for my wallet and took out a two-hundred-kwacha bill that I gave to the girl.

"Bring the change to me. I need some tambalas for tea."

"*Enya ŵadada* (yes father)," she answered.

My uncle gave her one of his huge smiles. The little girl skirted away.

"It's good you came to see us son. I'm broke because of that fool in your Benz there. I even bought him a ticket to take him to Lilongwe. Imagine!"

"So how did he reach Blantyre?"

"How can you ask me such a question? We're grown-ups, aren't we?"

He brought his hands together and rested them on his protruded belly which pushed through his white shirt. He seemed to fill the goatskin-covered chair with his whole frame. I felt my breath shorten. Goodson Gondwe sucked all the air around him; it was no hidden fact. He also sucked all the food and drink in the household so much so that the fatter he grew, the thinner the people and animals around him became. I briefly wondered where this growth would stop.

"Where is *ŵamama?*" I asked. Her presence suddenly became indispensable to my survival.

"*Ha,* that woman. Useless woman. She's not back from the borehole," he answered with nonchalance. His mocking grin grew wider and I thought he would laugh in the end, but he didn't. Then he added as an afterthought: "We killed a hyena yesterday."

The orange glow that had accompanied me up to his hut had long faded into the background. In its place, fiery rays of a melting sun cast ethereal shadows on Mr. Gondwe's encroaching figure. He still had the same bulbous eyes that used to frighten me when I was a teenager living under his roof. They still made me uneasy after all those years away from home. I tried as much as I could never to cross their path. They were now boring into my whole being.

"So," he roared. "What brought you here my son?"

"I came to fetch Vinjeru's clothes and schoolbooks. He said that he'd left them here," I said, standing up and picking up the car keys.

"*Ha, ha, ha!* You came all the way to Rumphi to get some rags. You educated boys will never cease to surprise me."

He disappeared into the house and came back a few minutes later with a plastic bag filled with a dark brown thin blanket that smelt of sweat and urine.

"Is this what you were looking for? *Ha, ha, ha!* My boy, all the way to Kanena to fetch this! So you have not changed, even with your pile of certificates and degrees. You're still the same stupid boy I remember. Help me God before I do something bad to you. Get out of my sight."

With trembling hands, I took the bag from him, all the while avoiding his belittling grin. He stepped closer to my chair and patted my back.

"You will never change. Cowards die a thousand deaths."

His last words lingered in my mind on my way back to the Mercedes but not for long. I soon embraced the quiet comfort of the Benz and was glad when the engine came to life. I pulled away from the rocky yard under the penetrating gaze of Goodson Gondwe, the proud owner of Gondwe and Sons' Investments. Vinjeru groaned and I told him to shut up.

THE END

VOCABULARY

1. <u>**DEFINITIONS (VERBS)**</u>**: Find the meanings of the following Verbs in a unilingual Dictionary.**

a. To dump:...

....

b. To claim:...

....

c. To cringe:...

....

d. To whimper:...

....

e. To stare:...

....

f. To mumble:...

....

g. To shrug:...

....

h. To stagger:...

....

i. To retch:...

....

j. To groan:...

....

2. **<u>DEFINITIONS (NOUNS)</u>: Find the meanings of the following Nouns in a unilingual Dictionary.**

a. Complacency: ....

....

b. Remorse:.......................................

....

c. Disbelief: ....

....

d. Fascination: ....

....

e. Dismay:..

....

f. Lunacy:..

....

g. Admonishment:..................................

....

h. Ordeal:..

....

i. Cadence:.......................................

....

j. Leniency: ....

....

k. Survival: ....

....

3. <u>SYNONYMS:</u> Find the words that have the same meaning as the Verbs below.

Word	Synonym	Word	Synonym
To tighten		To start	
To hide		To stutter	
To writhe		To slow down	
To retreat		To hiss	
To ask		To answer	
To pick		To disappear	

4. <u>ANTONYMS:</u> Find the words that have the opposite meaning of the Adjectives below.

Word	Antonym	Word	Antonym
Soaked		Nervous	
Hard		Continuous	
Sharp		Thick	
Bizarre		Painful	
Irate		Grotesque	
Mad		Educated	

5. <u>**WORD SEARCH:**</u> **Vocabulary in 'The Pinnacle of Irresponsibility'.**

```
G P V D I S E D E C R E M Q K
T O Y W K U Z T T E L L A W Y
Q Z D U J J Q G N R X H P B J
K S I S H Y E N A H C U U M R
S K B A Q A I C T Z B J R Z A
J P T R A W D L N N E T L F S
E S L U D A A L U W L X S U K
R D I A M E S U O H L Z N E B
I K E P W B G F C H I S E L P
C R O A D B L O C K E E D T R
B N E P H E W E A T S S R C S
X Y J Y B A J R R T D D U N A
W O K G R O W T H F E K B O X
U J L D H I O R U V L O W T H
R G S S L C S T N Z W L I S E
```

ACCOUNTANT	HOUSEHOLD
BELLIES	HOUSEMAID
BENZ	HYENA
BOOT	MERCEDES
BREADWINNER	NEPHEW
BURDENS	ROAD BLOCK
COWARDS	SUNSET
FUEL	TUMBLER
GAZE	WALLET
GOAT	WEALTH
GROWTH	

6. <u>MAIN THEMES:</u> The words below are related to a particular theme in the short story. Can you classify them in the table below?

dogs, thief, uniform, shove, night guard, uncle, leash, snake, prey, power, mangled, boys, disobeyed, coward, housemaid, branding, belittling, pounce, stuttering, punch, retreated, soft, disappeared, cover, employer, houseboy, breadwinner, goat, present, owner, thousands, bribes, afraid, cowards, protruded, boy, frighten

Greed	Authority	Cowardice	Dehumanisation

7. **WRITING: Write sentences using the following expressions.**

a. Bear witness to something: . . . .

. . . .

. . . .

b. To tighten one's grip around something: . . . .

. . . .

. . . .

c. To be thirsty for revenge: . . . .

. . . .

. . . .

d. To writhe in pain: . . . .

. . . .

. . . .

e. To live in the shadow of something: . . . .

. . . .

. . . .

f. To goad someone into doing something: . . . .

. . . .

. . . .

g. To shrug one's shoulders: . . . .

. . . .

. . . .

GENERAL COMPREHENSION

1. **GENERAL COMPREHENSION: Read the short story once again and answer the questions below.**

a. What is the title of the short story?: . . . .

. . . .

. . . .

b. What is the story about?: . . . .

. . . .

. . . .

c. Imagine another title for the short story: . . . .

. . . .

. . . .

d. Who is the narrator?: . . . .

e. How old is he or she?: . . . .

f. Describe the narrator in a few words.: . . . .

. . . .

. . . .

g. Where does the story take place?: . . . .

h. What are the other places that are mentioned in the story?: . . . .

. . . .

. . . .

i. Pick out two other major characters in the short story and describe them: . . . .

. . . .

. . . .

DETAILED COMPREHENSION

2. **DETAILED COMPREHENSION: Read the short story once again, paying closer attention to how it was written, and answer the questions below.**
TRUE OR FALSE: Say if the following sentences are TRUE or FALSE. Justify your answer.

a. The narrator agrees with what the night guard is doing.:

. . . .

. . . .

b. The boy is a thief.: . . . .

. . . .

. . . .

c. The narrator's wife is very empathetic towards the boy.:

. . . .

. . . .

d. The narrator helps the boy in his own way.: . . . .

. . . .

. . . .

e. The narrator's uncle is a kind man.: . . . .

. . . .

. . . .

f. The narrator is a coward.: . . . .

. . . .

. . . .

. . . .

WRITE FULL ANSWERS TO THE FOLLOWING QUESTIONS:

a. How can you characterize the narrator's behaviour at the beginning of the story?: . . . .

. . . .

. . . .

. . . .

b. Does the narrator behave the same way at the end of the story?: . . . .

. . . .

. . . .

. . . .

c. What can you say about the night guard's behaviour?:

. . . .

. . . .

. . . .

d. How does the narrator's wife treat the boy? . . . .

. . . .

. . . .

. . . .

e. What is the role of a housemaid in the story? How does she react when she sees her employer?: . . . .

. . . .

. . . .

. . . .

f. What is the narrator's attitude towards his job?: . . . . . .

. . . .

. . . .

. . . .

g. Who is the narrator's uncle? Where does he live? How can you describe this man?: ....

    ....

    ....

    ....

    ....

h. Give a brief description of the village where the uncle lives.: ....

    ....

    ....

    ....

    ....

i. Describe the narrator's relationship with his uncle.:

    ....

    ....

    ....

    ....

j. What does the uncle say about the boy?: ....

    ....

    ....

    ....

k. What does the narrator say about his visit to the village? ....

    ....

    ....

    ....

l. What should the narrator have said or done instead?:

    ....

    ....

    ....

WRITTEN EXPRESSION

3. **REWRITE THE STORY: Rewrite the short story. All the characters will behave differently towards the boy.**

PAY ATTENTION TO THE FOLLOWING POINTS:

a. **Plot or Structure:** Think about how your story unfolds and develops in time. What will be the.....?:

Exposition:...

Rising action:..

Climax:...

Falling action: ....

Resolution:...

b. **Vocabulary:** Avoid repeating words unless it is a deliberate, stylistic device. Use descriptive language and show instead of telling.

c. **Grammar:** Pay attention to how you write. Think about tenses, syntax, spelling and punctuation.

d. **Originality:** Make your story as interesting as possible. It should be worth the read.

WRITTEN EXPRESSION CHECKLIST	
My story has a title.	✓
My story has a plot.	✓
I have varied the vocabulary.	✓
I have paid attention to grammar (tenses, syntax, spelling and punctuation.)	✓
My story is original and interesting.	✓

NOTES